SEATTLE STYLE
FASHION/ FUNCTION

SEATTLE STYLE
FASHION/ FUNCTION

Museum of History & Industry

Curated by Clara Berg

CONTENTS

FOREWORD

To me, "Seattle style" is a poetic juxtaposition. The contrast of our constantly growing cityscape against mountains and interconnected waters creates interest and intrigue. Our unique urban environment surrounded by nature has a soft-spoken, understated beauty. It has inspired my work since the beginning. It inspires me even more so today.

Seemingly low-key and laid-back, Seattle style is at the forefront of innovation and technology. We are a cool hotbed of industry leaders—think Alaska Airlines, Amazon, Microsoft, Boeing, and Starbucks, among many others. Our city's energy has been known to be a catalyst for new ideas, generating distinct sparks for inventive thinking. Perpetually remaking itself, Seattle attracts all kinds, from adventurers to academics and beyond. We are changing the world, elevating the human experience, and making history together.

Transformative with purpose, my designs are also influenced by our weather. It generates an emotional temperature encouraging layers of color and texture. Beside the beautiful shades of our skies, I love how objects and colors appear more vibrant here. Over time, Seattle has helped shape my collections. I like to embed hidden, unexpected details that give a sense of discovery—whether it is in couture for one or uniforms for thousands. Living within this beautiful environment evokes emotions that inspire us to be the best versions of ourselves.

The foundation of great design comes from a perfect balance of form and function, affecting people in a positive way every day.

— Luly Yang

Luly Yang, designer and creative director of Luly Yang Couture, wearing one of her designs. Photo: Lisa Town

INTRODUCTION

Does Seattle have style? Many seem eager to answer no—saying Seattle is too outdoorsy, too provincial, too casual, or simply uninterested. Yet, a scratch to the surface reveals Seattleites who care deeply about what they wear. They include everyone from outdoor adventurers keenly aware that the right clothing can be a lifeline, to fashion devotees going to great lengths to bring chic treasures back home, to those who want to change narratives around what we wear. Grunge may be the style most associated with Seattle, but its ingredients—utilitarian needs, casual dressing, and a nonconformist attitude—resonate in many Seattle clothing stories before and since. No single style defines this region.

Seattle Style: Fashion/Function features highlights from the Museum of History & Industry's clothing and accessory collection, ranging from the mid-1800s to today. When we look at the clothing made and worn here, enduring and distinct influences are revealed: the climate and natural surroundings, the city's aspiration to grow from a frontier town to a major metropolis, a local affinity for casualwear, and a spirit of people forging a new path. Alone, few of these ingredients are unique to Seattle. But when they are woven together, a distinct Seattle story emerges.

Some of the pieces highlighted in this catalog favor function, each feature serving a practical need. Others are pure fashion, a flourish of elegance and artistic energy. Most are somewhere in between, combining pragmatic needs with a flair for self-expression. After all, the very nature of clothing balances personal needs—comfort, fit, warmth, texture—with how we want to look and be perceived by others.

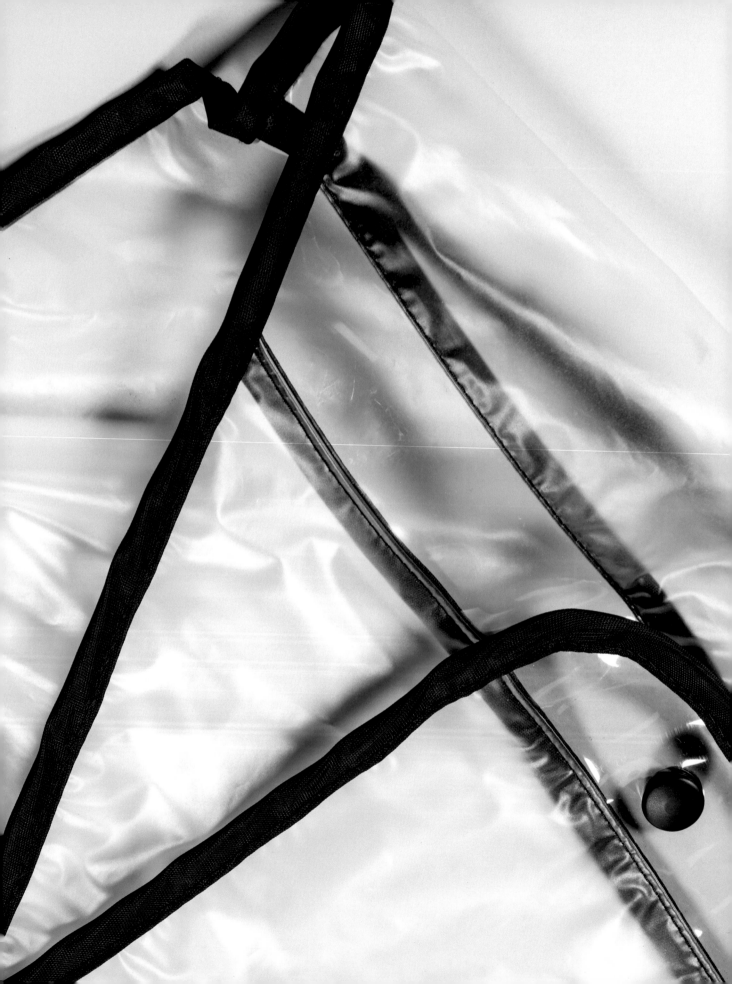

NATURE AND PLACE

Water surrounds Seattle on the east and west, and snowcapped mountains are within sight of downtown. Here, the adventure of the great outdoors feels within reach. An average of 150 days of rain each year feeds lush forests; it also makes the damp climate a part of daily life.

Dressing according to the weather in this region is a thousands-year-old practice begun by Native peoples, Seattle's original inhabitants. The Duwamish, Suquamish, and other surrounding Coast Salish tribes have used locally sourced materials like cedar bark and wool for garments. This clothing keeps wearers warm and dry but also incorporates artistic creativity in hereditary designs. Seattle's passion for blending weather-tested textiles with visual impact continues with traditional materials, as well as new ones like waxed cotton, Gore-Tex, and vinyl.

Today, the natural world and the urban environment are in constant conversation. Seattle's clothing—what has been made and worn here—demonstrates this influence in a combination of practical versatility and sophisticated styling. From the hardiest of gear to an elegant evening coat, Seattleites are ready for a life outdoors, whether it be on the city street or the mountain trail.

Colette raincoat (detail).

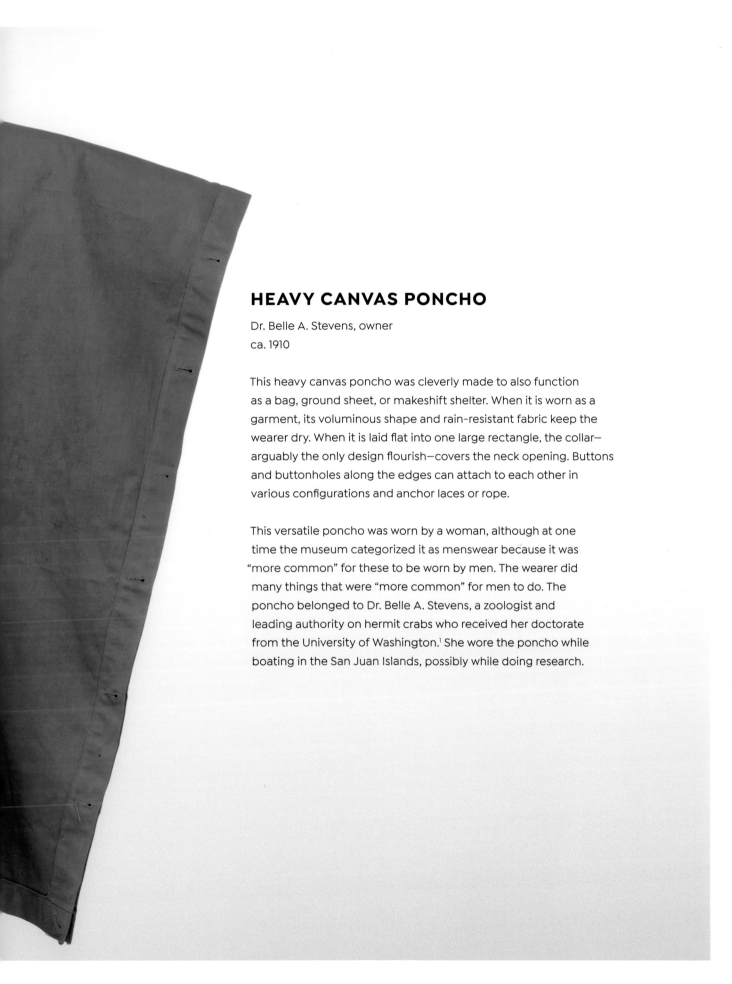

HEAVY CANVAS PONCHO

Dr. Belle A. Stevens, owner
ca. 1910

This heavy canvas poncho was cleverly made to also function as a bag, ground sheet, or makeshift shelter. When it is worn as a garment, its voluminous shape and rain-resistant fabric keep the wearer dry. When it is laid flat into one large rectangle, the collar— arguably the only design flourish—covers the neck opening. Buttons and buttonholes along the edges can attach to each other in various configurations and anchor laces or rope.

This versatile poncho was worn by a woman, although at one time the museum categorized it as menswear because it was "more common" for these to be worn by men. The wearer did many things that were "more common" for men to do. The poncho belonged to Dr. Belle A. Stevens, a zoologist and leading authority on hermit crabs who received her doctorate from the University of Washington.[1] She wore the poncho while boating in the San Juan Islands, possibly while doing research.

HIKING BOOTS

Recreational Equipment Inc. (REI), retailer
Leila Martin, owner
1967

Recreational Equipment Inc. (REI) imported these hiking boots from Switzerland to sell in its Seattle store. They were worn by Seattleite Leila Martin, who recalled that owning such an expensive pair of boots just for hiking felt like a luxury. Despite this, she was uncomfortable wearing them in even the most casual restaurant en route to a climb—she always brought a pair of street shoes along. Martin wore these boots to climb Mount Rainier in 1970.

Lloyd and Mary Anderson founded REI in 1938 as a way to get better gear for climbing. They formed the co-op to buy high-quality gear from Europe in large, cost-effective batches with friends from the Mountaineers, a local club devoted to outdoor recreation, education, and preservation. Today, REI sells its own in-house lines of clothing and gear in addition to top brands from around the world.

REI founders Mary and Lloyd Anderson pose in climbing gear, December 15, 1946.

EARLY GORE-TEX RAIN JACKET

Mountain Safety Research, maker
ca. 1976

This jacket has two features familiar to most Seattleites today: rainproof Gore-Tex fabric and zippered underarm vents. Seattle-based company Mountain Safety Research (MSR) was one of the first to make use of Gore-Tex for recreational wear. Unlike most waterproof fabrics before it, Gore-Tex uses a special membrane layer laminated to the inside of the shell fabric, rather than using a chemical coating on the fabric's surface. The result is something lightweight, flexible, windproof, and breathable.[2] MSR was also the first to introduce underarm vents called *pit zips*.[3] Unglamorous perhaps, but pit zips are an ingenious solution to the sweaty jacket conundrum, without sacrificing protection from the elements.

This jacket, owned by an employee of MSR, was test worn before Gore-Tex jackets went into general production. Initially, jackets like this one were worn strictly for outdoor adventures. But later in the 20th century, pricey high-tech gear became a Seattle status symbol—appropriate for daily wear in the city.

This 1976 photo shows the two-way zippered vents on a similar MSR jacket. Another MSR innovation, the Thunderbird ice axe, can also be seen. MSR founder, engineer and mountaineer Larry Penberthy, was dedicated to creating safe, innovative climbing gear.[4] Photo: MSR

HUNTING JACKET AND BREECHES

Filson, maker
ca. 1922

This outfit combines two classic Filson pieces: laced breeches and a hunting jacket. The breeches are reinforced at the seat and on the front of the thighs for walking or riding. The hunting jacket features four types of pockets used for storing everything from a compass to game. The pocket for storing game can be accessed from the front of the jacket, and leads to a large cavity within the back. One small pocket's placement is a mystery, however. It is uncommon to have one on the upper right shoulder, where the gun usually rests. Filson frequently customized orders, so it may have been a special request. One explanation is that this jacket was used for some outdoor activity other than hunting.

For a century, Filson has served those who labor outdoors professionally as well as those whose adventures are pure passion. A 1914 catalog describes the brand as making garments for miners, lumbermen, sportsmen, and explorers.[5]

The cover of Filson's 1922 catalog features a similar outfit. Photo: Filson

HIKING OUTFIT

Queen City, maker
1920s

This two-piece ensemble includes a pair of short pants or *knickers*—
a new option for women's hiking clothing in the late 1910s and
early 1920s. The pockets are functional, and a roomy cut in the seat
makes for easy movement.

In the 1920s, women's fashion made revolutionary steps. The young
woman of the period, the "flapper," is today mostly associated with
shockingly short evening gowns with beading and fringe. But these
rebellious and energetic women also broke ground in daywear and
sportswear—daring to go adventuring in knickers instead of long skirts,
or hitting the beach in clingy knit bathing suits. As a 1919 editorial in the
Seattle Times explained, "The girl who puts on a pair of knickerbockers
and a golf jacket and goes out for a 10-mile hike with her brother or
her sweetheart doesn't look half as pretty as her mother did . . . but
[she] is the one who's having the good times these days."[6]

A similar outfit for "rough
outings" was shown as part
of a Rhodes Department
Store ad (right), in the
Seattle Times in 1926.
Knickers were worn with
tall socks to cover bare
skin below the knee.
Drawing: *Seattle Times*,
May 26, 1926, page 9

WOOL SKI ENSEMBLE

Seattle Woolen Company, maker
ca. 1948

Like many ski ensembles, this one nods to both function and fashion—fitting for the slopes as well as the lodge. It is made from dense, warm wool. The knitted cuffs on the jacket and pants keep snow out and make it easier to put on gloves and boots. But the patterned mittens, yellow pocket button, and the wide pant leg give it a stylish air.

This ensemble was made, in part, by the Seattle Woolen Company, which began with a focus on menswear and water-repellent garments to appeal to "woodsmen, cannery workers, and fishermen."[7] They soon expanded to include clothing for sport and recreation, and began making more options for women. As it became increasingly acceptable for women to participate in sporting activities, local companies met the demand. In the 1940s, Seattle Woolen Company began advertising their line of "Terrain Tested Ski Clothing from Ski Country" for both men and women.[8]

Previous: Skiers at Snoqualmie Pass, 1938.

ONE-PIECE SKI SUIT

Roffe Inc., maker
1980s

Brightly colored one-piece ski suits were a hot style in the 1980s. This one has snaps that are color-matched and thoughtfully placed to not interrupt the lines where colors intersect. Each snap has an *R* for Roffe.

Sam Roffe founded the company in Seattle in 1953, after spending 22 years as a cutter at Seattle Woolen. Roffe himself was never a skier, but he had a passion for craftsmanship and ingenuity, and enjoyed assisting on the manufacturing floor. The company designed the United States Ski Team uniforms for the 1964 Olympics, giving Roffe global exposure.[9] In 1967, Roffe hired experienced skier Wini Jones as lead designer. Jones innovated new concepts and designs throughout her 30 years at Roffe.[10] By the 1980s, Roffe Inc. was the largest skiwear manufacturer in the US.[11]

Roffe Inc. became famous in the 1960s for being the first US manufacturer of stretch ski pants. This promotional photo shows an example from 1983.

WOOL EVENING COAT

J. S. Graham, retailer
ca. 1890

This elaborate wool coat would be warm enough for a Seattle winter, but fancy enough to wear for an evening at the theater. By the late 19th century, Seattle had several theaters and opera houses to warrant such a formal coat. This was purchased from pioneer retailer J. S. Graham, which opened just after the Great Seattle Fire of 1889.[12]

J. S. Graham was a women's specialty store that touted its connection to the latest styles from afar. In the 1890s, J. S. Graham advertised a stock that included "Imported Costumes" from Paris and Berlin.[13] The store's labels emphasized its connections to Paris as well as London. Newspapers noted owner John Graham traveled to New York to select goods for the store.[14] The exceptional workmanship of this coat suggests it was one of these imports—a piece that would bring prestige and clout to the store by its very presence.

The complex construction of this coat is most evident in the elegant pleating at the back.

OVERCOAT WITH CAPE

John Doyle Bishop, owner
ca. 1970

This coat references classic 19th-century *greatcoat* and *ulster* overcoat styles. It is long and double-breasted, and its notched collar can fold over the neck for extra warmth. The most important reference, however, is the cape. A wool cape resists rain and directs water off the shoulders. It can also flip up to be used as a hood. This coat has practical aspects, but the color and contrasting plaid and checkered patterns are pure style. The late 1960s saw a resurgence of color and pattern in men's clothing, known as the "peacock revolution." Some devotees added references to Romantic and Edwardian styles such as frilled cravats and heavy brocade jackets.

From 1950 to 1980, John Doyle Bishop was a leading tastemaker in Seattle, known for the elegant clothing sold at his eponymous store. He was also known for his flamboyant personality and distinct style of dressing.[15] Bishop put a label from his own store in this coat, decorated with shamrocks to celebrate his Irish American heritage.

Fashion illustration from England showing an ulster overcoat, 1903. Photo: Public domain

FAIRWEATHER RAINCOAT

Totem Sportswear, maker
1962

"Fairweather" may seem like a strange name for a raincoat. This coat is made from a light, waterproofed cotton, so the name could refer to those balmy rainy days that have only a light sprinkle—"fair" weather by Seattle standards. It likely also refers to the World's Fair Seattle hosted from April to October of 1962.

Seattle's Totem Sportswear made this raincoat in their South Lake Union factory. In 1962, a snappy reversible Totem coat was named as the official "All Purpose Coat" of the World's Fair.[16] Totem was so proud of this achievement, it was noted on labels of other coats released the same year, including this one. Like many local companies, they were eager to capitalize on the influx of visitors and national attention. Nearly 10 million people visited the 1962 World's Fair—more than the combined population of Washington, Oregon, Alaska, and British Columbia at the time.

Previous: Fair visitors, dressed for a rainy day, in front of the Republic of China Pavilion, 1962.

![clear coated logo]

COLETTE RAINCOAT

Clear Coated, maker
2018

The idea for Clear Coated raincoats came from an all-too-familiar Seattle experience. Seattle designer Miriam Reynolds Rigby tired of countless days dressing up in an interesting outfit, only to cover it up with a dreary raincoat. She was inspired to create a new incarnation of the classic clear raincoat, which had been popular at various times in the 20th century. A see-through coat protects from the rain while keeping the outfit underneath in full view. Rigby's "Colette" design features sets of snaps, arranged in a triangle, to allow for a narrower or wider fit. The cuffs can be wide or snap closely to the wrist. She created the first version of her Clear Coated raincoat as part of a final project while attending a leading apparel design program at Seattle Central College.

The original intention was to highlight the clothing under the coat. However, the futuristic aesthetic of Clear Coated's rainwear is visually striking in its own right.

The snaps are cleverly placed to close two ways—creating either a tighter shape as shown on the mannequin, or wider as shown here. Photo: Julia Bruk for Clear Coated

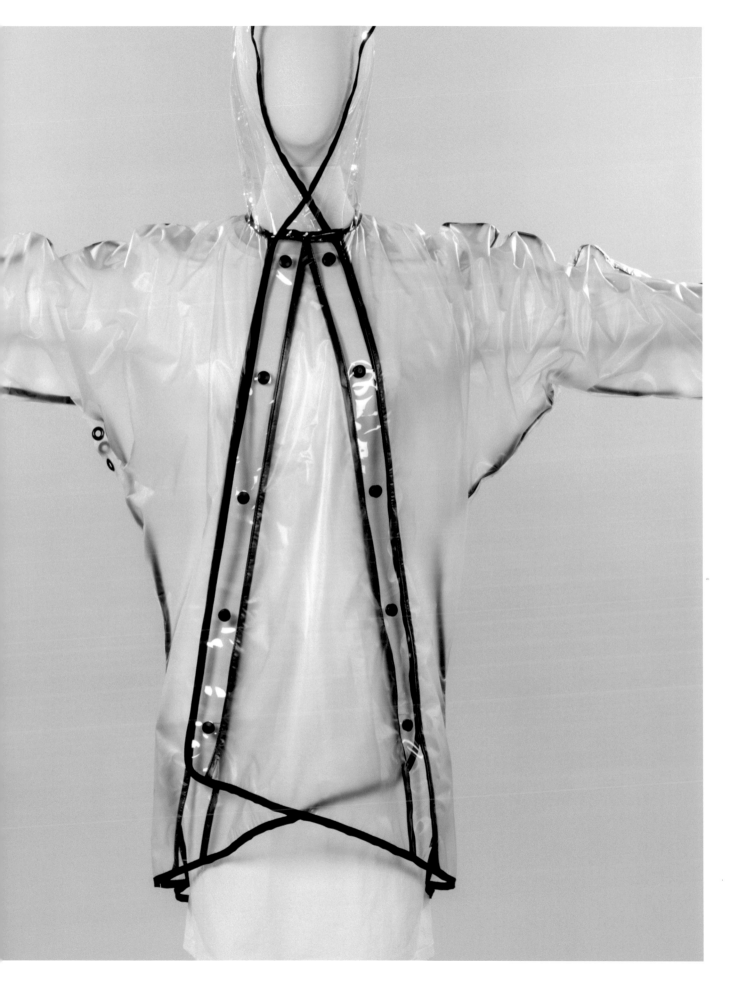

GROWTH AND ASPIRATION

When Seattle was a frontier town—little more than a collection of houses and muddy streets—its residents imagined a future when the site would be home to a global metropolis. The first name for the settlement was "New York Alki," *alki* meaning "by and by" or "in the future" in the local trade language of Chinook Jargon. Becoming a city has meant periods of rapid growth and transformative change—the two seem to have become part of Seattle's DNA.

As the town grew in size, prominent community members developed cultural organizations that would add the clout and sophistication of a metropolis. Seattleites also looked to fashion as a barometer of cosmopolitan success, the presence of and access to fashionable goods used as a measure of connections and taste.

Dynamics of aspiration and growth are reflected in the clothing worn here. Despite its youth and remote location, Seattle has always been a place where money could be made. Early fortunes were made in logging, fishing, real estate, and railways. Between 1890 and 1900, Seattle's population almost doubled, fueled by the Klondike Gold Rush. Population booms bring new workers, wealth, and talent. The 21st-century tech boom is pushing Seattle's population to new limits. From 2010 to 2017, Seattle was the fastest-growing big city in the US.[1] This kind of growth shapes the population and its needs, which in turn influence local stores and companies.

Cellular automata knit scarf (detail).

WOOL MACKINAW CRUISER JACKET

Filson, maker
2013

The "Mackinaw Cruiser" jacket was designed for timber *cruisers*—workers who measure trees and collect forest data. The back has a double layer of wool for warmth and to accommodate a roomy back pocket for storing maps. Filson patented the "Mackinaw Cruiser" in 1914. The same coat is still in production today with only a few modifications.

Between 1897 and 1900 an estimated 100,000 prospectors headed to the Yukon for the Klondike Gold Rush. Seattle was the embarkation point for almost two-thirds of them, and so local merchants clamored to "mine the miners" by selling supplies.[2] Filson was founded in 1897 to outfit the miners for the harsh conditions of the north. The *Mackinaw* fabric—a term for heavy, dense wool—was one of the first products Clinton C. Filson advertised. He made blankets, coats, and boot insulation out of the durable and warm material.[3] Filson built a reputation for quality goods, one his company has sustained into the 21st century.

The "Mackinaw Cruiser" jacket as it appeared in Filson's 1922 catalog. Throughout its tenure, the jacket has been used for different reasons by a variety of customer types—from deer hunters who appreciate the bright red color to those who simply have an affinity for plaid. Photo: Filson

HEELED BOOTS

Wallin & Nordstrom, retailer
1901–29

These early 20th-century boots have an unusually modern detail: rather than closing with a series of buttons or laces, a strap wraps around the ankle and snaps in place. The boots are from Wallin & Nordstrom, the earliest incarnation of the powerhouse fashion retailer Nordstrom, still in business today.

John Nordstrom met Carl Wallin during the Gold Rush. The two reconnected in Seattle and decided to go into business together with money Nordstrom made in the Klondike.[4] In 1901, they opened the Wallin & Nordstrom shoe store, which carried a full range of "fashionable, sensible, comfortable, and durable" shoes for adults and children.[5] The "Wallin" name was dropped in the late 1920s, when both original partners retired and sold their shares to Nordstrom's sons. Nordstrom continued as a shoes-only business until 1963, when they purchased Best's Apparel, a higher-end women's clothing store in Seattle.

Carl Wallin (left) and John Nordstrom (right) outside the first Wallin & Nordstrom shoe store at 318 Pike Street, about 1901.

```
// processing sketch, modded by fbz from an
example from processing book
// 1d elementary cellular automata with
tiff saving ability
// handy script for output on a knitting
machine
// type code into Processing, a free coding
language and environment:
https://processing.org

int[] rules = { 0, 1, 0, 1, 1, 0, 1, 0 };
//which rule would you like? this is rule
90 in binary
int gen = 1; // generation
color on = color(255);
color off = color(0);

void setup() {
  size(98, 1090); // width, length
  //frameRate(8); // slowdown to 8 frames
each second
  background(0);
  //set(width-1, 0, on); //set the next to
last pixel to on, handy for rule 110
  set(13, 0, on); //turn on a pixel for the
seed row
  set(37, 0, on);
  set(67, 0, on);
  set(79, 0, on);
  set(84, 0, on);
  set(87, 0, on);
  set(93, 0, on); //turn on another pixel
for the seed row
}

void draw() {
// for each pixel, determine new state by
examining current state
// and neighbor states and ignore edges
that have only one neighbor
  for (int i = 1; i < width - 1; i++) {
    int left = get(i - 1, gen - 1);  //
left neighbor
    int me = get(i, gen - 1);         //
current pixel
    int right = get(i + 1, gen - 1); //
right neighbor
    if (rules(left, me right) == 1) {
      set(i, gen, on);
    }
  }
  gen++; // increment the generation by 1
  if (gen > height - 1) { // if it reaches
the bottom of the screen,
    noLoop();               // stop the
program
  }
  save("knityak_rule90_788.tif");  //save a
tiff image of output in sketch folder,
rename to save multiple
}
// implement the rules
int rules(color a, color b, color c) {
  if ((a == on) && (b == on) && (c == on))
{
    return rules[0];
  }
  if ((a == on) && (b == on) && (c == off))
{
    return rules[1];
  }
  if ((a == on) && (b = off) && (c == on))
{
    return rules[2];
  }
  if ((a == on) && (b == off) && (c ==
off)) {
    return rules[3];
  }
  if ((a == off) && (b == on) && (c == on))
{
    return rules[4];
  }
  if ((a == off) && (b == on) && (c ==
off)) {
    return rules[5];
  }
  if ((a == off) && (b == off) && (c ==
on)) {
    return rules[6];
  }
  if ((a == off) && (b == off) && (c ==
off)) {
    return rules[7];
  }
  return 0;
}
```

CELLULAR AUTOMATA KNIT SCARF

KnitYak, maker

2018

KnitYak combines industrial knitting with inventive computer programming. Most beginning programmers learn the *elementary cellular automata* code, yet it outputs seemingly complex visual structures—as seen in this scarf. Each stitch acts like a screen pixel: black and white stitches represent binary 0s and 1s. KnitYak's work echoes a historic relationship between textile design and computer technology. One of the first uses for binary code was to program looms to weave elaborate patterns.

Seattle has a computer-and-tech-oriented culture, thanks in part to giants like Microsoft and Amazon. The current tech boom feeds this community by drawing a population of talent, including programmer Fabienne Serrière. Serrière first experimented with knitting by hacking small consumer knitting machines. In 2015, she launched KnitYak and bought an industrial knitting machine capable of complex, programmable designs—no hacking needed. Those within the computer-and-tech community are KnitYak's biggest clients. This scarf's pattern is recognizable to people familiar with the elementary cellular automata code.

Every scarf comes with its code. This scarf used Rule 90 of the 256 rules of the elementary cellular automata. Rule 90 is related to Sierpinski triangles, the fractal triangle pattern discovered by the mathematician of the same name. Photo: KnitYak

EVENING BONNET

Mrs. Edwin Bowden, owner
1888

As Seattle grew, two factors influenced the availability of fashionable goods. One was connection, which depended on the available routes for stylish items to be transported to Seattle and the level of access to fashion news. The second was need, which depended on the types of events occurring in Seattle that required new and fashionable garments.

The bonnet belonged to Mrs. Edwin Bowden, who came to Seattle in 1882. From 1884 to 1889, the Frye Opera House served as Seattle's premier cultural attraction for an expanding population.[6] In anticipation of an upcoming performance by soprano Emma Abbott at the Frye Opera House, Bowden ordered this fashionable hat from New York. It arrived, likely by train, in a wooden box after anxious waiting on Bowden's part, just in time to be worn to the performance. Transcontinental train service reached Washington in the 1880s—a trip that once took months could now be made in less than a week. Quicker access to fashions from New York and San Francisco dampened Seattle's need to build a local high fashion industry.

Feathers, and sometimes even the entire bird, were popular hat trimming in the late 19th century. The craze nearly drove some bird species to extinction. The devastation prompted the first federal law to protect wildlife, the Lacey Act of 1900.

CHIFFON AND TAFFETA DRESS

Harry Collins, Morry and George Schulman, New York, makers
MacDougall & Southwick, retailer
ca. 1915

This light and romantic dress is typical of 1910s fashion. The wide hips reference the 18th century, but the shortened length is evidence of the modernizing changes that occurred during the First World War.

The labels on this gown hint at the long journey that fashionable items took to Seattle. Influential New York designer Harry Collins created an original version of this dress. A ready-to-wear firm in New York then bought the rights to copy and distribute the design. Next, a buyer from MacDougall & Southwick—who likely travelled multiple times a year to fashion capitals like New York and Paris—brought the dress to Seattle.

MacDougall & Southwick was one of Seattle's earliest department stores, tracing its roots back to a shop that opened in 1875.[7] In 1907, it sent its first delegation of buyers to Europe.[8]

The grand Toklas & Singerman building at Front Street (First Avenue) and Columbia Street, in 1888, just before it was destroyed in the Great Seattle Fire. Before a change of ownership, MacDougall & Southwick was known as Toklas & Singerman.

DRESS AND JACKET ENSEMBLE

The Bon Marché, retailer
Rona, New York, maker
ca. 1964

This crisp green dress and jacket are from The Bon Marché, one of Seattle's largest and most influential department stores. The ensemble is simple but has a few striking details, including the triangular arrangement of the buttons on the jacket and the padded roll around the dress collar to frame the wearer's neck. It was purchased from the "Northwest Room," the department for the highest-end designer fashions. Department stores like The Bon gave more people greater access to goods from afar. The Northwest Room did not refer to where clothes were from. Rather, it suggested a go-to spot for Northwest women to be elegantly dressed. This ensemble was designed and made in New York.

Edward and Josephine Nordhoff founded The Bon Marché in 1890. They were inspired by the famed Paris department store Le Bon Marché (meaning "the good deal").[9] The Bon continued into the 21st century until it was renamed as part of the Macy's brand.

Co-founder of The Bon Marché, Josephine Nordhoff McDermott, about 1900. When Edward died in 1899, Josephine steered the business into the 20th century. She was an early advocate of the eight-hour workday.

DELPHOS GOWN

Mariano Fortuny, Italy, maker
Zoë Dusanne, owner
ca. 1920

Mariano Fortuny and his wife Henriette first created finely pleated "Delphos" gowns in 1907. It was an unabashedly modernist look because the dress could be worn without a corset. The design was so forward thinking that Fortuny was able to produce and sell versions of the gown until his death in 1949.

It is fitting that this dress came to the museum collection through Zoë Dusanne. Dusanne was herself a forward-thinking modernist and Seattle's first professional modern art dealer. She exhibited cutting-edge European artists in the art gallery she opened in 1950.[10] Dusanne was also a strong advocate for local contemporary artists such as Mark Tobey and Paul Horiuchi. She left an indelible mark on culture in Seattle. The dress was a gift to Dusanne from New York–based artist Charmion von Wiegand. Purple was Dusanne's signature color.[11]

Zoë Dusanne photographed in the early 1920s. Photo: University of Washington Libraries, Special Collections, UW 28849

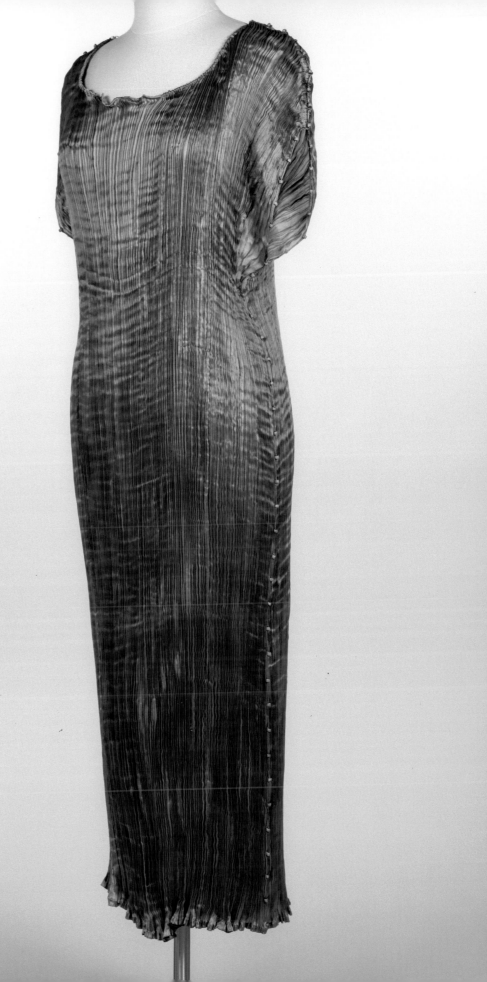

VELVET EVENING GOWN

Mrs. George T. Myers, owner
ca. 1927

The width of this evening dress afforded the designer an opportunity to showcase an elaborate beaded pattern. Small-sized garments predominate in museum collections, so this dress is rare. Clothing and fabric used to be much more expensive. Garments were commonly reused, restyled, and remade many times. Items too small to rework or be passed on to another family member were more likely to stay in their original condition. Because more smaller-sized garments survived, an inaccurate perception has been created that people were smaller in the past. Fashion historians call this theory *survival bias*. This dress may have been saved by its beading—any reduction of the size would require butchering the pattern.

The dress belonged to Mrs. George T. Myers, whose family did well in the salmon canning business. She was a prominent supporter of several charities including Children's Hospital and Lighthouse for the Blind.

SILK EVENING GOWN

Elsa Schiaparelli, Paris, maker
Guendolen Plestcheeff, owner
1937

The butterflies on this print are lifelike enough to have the surreal effect of covering the wearer in fluttering insects. Also surprising is the visible plastic zipper at the back of an otherwise sleek gown. Couture designer Elsa Schiaparelli was known for her adventurous and surrealist creations and was one of the first designers to use zippers as a prominent design element.

The gown belonged to Guendolen Carkeek Plestcheeff, who was born in Seattle but spent time in Europe as a young woman. She continued to make buying trips overseas to restock her wardrobe long after she moved back to Seattle in 1931. The buying trips did not go unnoticed. Plestcheeff was frequently cited as one of Seattle's best-dressed women, and this reputation extended far beyond the city.[12]

Plestcheeff would have worn this gown around the time that she was elected as president of the Seattle Historical Society in 1938. She was a major force in the opening of the society's museum in 1952—the Museum of History & Industry.

Guendolen Plestcheeff
photographed in Paris,
1931.

SEQUINED EVENING GOWN

Madame Thiry, owner and retailer
ca. 1929

This dress, with its short skirt and boldly graphic rectangles of shiny and matte sequins, seems to presage the youthful mod dresses of the 1960s. It bears a label from a Seattle shop run by Madame Thiry.

Louise Schwaebele Thiry was born in Paris and came west in the early 20th century. Her fashion career started as a side business—importing goods from Paris to sell in Alaska and Seattle for supplementary income. After she lost her husband in World War I, her business became a lifeline to support her and her young son Paul, a future prominent Seattle architect.[13] From her enduring, pronounced French accent to styling herself as "Madame," Thiry leveraged her Parisian pedigree to gain authority in Seattle's fashion scene. Her labels further emphasize the point with "Importer" and "Chez Mme. Thiry." Her shop imported clothes that could be sold as is, or used as inspiration to have something similar made.[14]

EVENING GOWN WITH LACE OVERLAY

Helen Igoe, owner
ca. 1911

This gown balances flashy elements—gold threads, vivid blue silk, sequins, and coils of iridescent blue metal—with a subdued overlayer of black lace. Wearer Helen Igoe was an unmarried woman in her early 40s. She could not be defined as an ingénue, matron, or widow, so she had to pick clothes that forged a new path.

The new path was "businesswoman." Igoe was one of the most influential and formidable fashion figures in early 20th-century Seattle. In 1907, she was sent on the first-ever buying trip from Seattle to Europe while working for the department store MacDougall & Southwick.[15] In 1910, she opened the Helen Igoe Shop for Women. The *Seattle Times* called her shop a "Fashion Innovation"—it brought a Paris-like shopping experience to Seattle.[16] Igoe continued travelling to Europe and New York to stock her shop with the latest high fashions. She quickly became known as the leading authority on fashionable dress in the city.

Helen Igoe (center) with client Edith Thackwell Young (left) and New York designer Louise Barnes Gallagher (right), about 1940. Young was the Seattle Art Museum's education director. Gallagher's designs were sold at Igoe's shop.

PATTERNED SUIT

John Doyle Bishop, owner
ca. 1970

This bold suit with contrasting green prints is an excellent representation of its captivating wearer. John Doyle Bishop was known in Seattle for his role as a fashion authority and for enthusiasm about his Irish American heritage. Bishop's own suits were custom made and finely tailored, often in attention-grabbing prints and colors. Green was his signature color, which he incorporated in small details or head-to-toe looks, like this one.

Bishop was once called "Seattle's leading fashion retailer" by *Women's Wear Daily*.[17] He took over Helen Igoe's shop, at the corner of Fifth Avenue and Union Street, after her retirement and renamed it after himself. Like Igoe, Bishop sold glamorous women's clothing and accessories from European and American designers. While other stores battled for customers, 70 percent of Bishop's clients bought all their apparel exclusively from him. Some of his clients referred to themselves as "John's girls." Their devotion to Bishop was even called a "high fashion cult" by one reporter.[18]

In 1967, Bishop was
named one of the 100
most fashionable men
in the world by *Men's
Bazaar.* The *Seattle Post-
Intelligencer* took this
photo of him in his
store to celebrate.

TWO-PIECE BALL GOWN

House of Schiaparelli, Paris, maker
Ruth Schoenfeld Blethen Clayburgh, owner
ca. 1951

This ball gown has a commanding presence. It pairs a massive skirt with a beaded pink bodice and *peplum*, a ruffle at the waist, which becomes long tails at the back. The gown is from the couture house of Elsa Schiaparelli, likely during Hubert de Givenchy's design tenure in the early 1950s. It boldly contrasts the black skirt and beading with Schiaparelli's signature color, "shocking pink." A gown with this impact and pedigree could only be worn to the most elegant of evening events, by someone not afraid to stand out.

The wearer, Ruth Schoenfeld Blethen Clayburgh, was a prominent arts patron who the *Seattle Times* once described as "equal parts generous and stylish."[19] Clayburgh attended and organized many of Seattle's most glamorous fundraising events—ones worthy of such a gown. She was a founder of PONCHO (Patrons of Northwest Civic, Cultural and Charitable Organizations) and was involved with the Seattle Symphony fundraiser, Symphoneve. Symphoneve featured an elaborate fashion show as the main entertainment.

SILK COCKTAIL DRESS

Emilio Pucci, Italy, maker
Frederick & Nelson, retailer
1970s

This dress has a simple shape, but precision lies in the details. When it is worn, the stripes on the cuffs line up exactly with the stripes on the drop waist. Italian designer Emilio Pucci was known for geometric and kaleidoscopic bright prints, and sleek silhouettes that were influenced by his background in sportswear.

The dress was purchased from the "Designer Room" at Seattle department store Frederick & Nelson. The Designer Room was the department with the highest-end fashions—selling couture from Europe and top American designers from New York to Los Angeles. Pucci was a Frederick & Nelson favorite. In 1962, he visited Seattle in person to preside over a presentation of his fashions at Symphoneve, an annual fundraiser sponsored by Frederick & Nelson.[20]

Pucci designs from the Frederick & Nelson Designer Room, 1970.

EVENING GOWN WITH TAFFETA BOW

Irene, Los Angeles, maker
Frederick & Nelson, retailer
ca. 1955

The dramatic taffeta sash on this evening gown ties into a bow large enough to be seen from the front. The designer, Irene Lentz, known professionally as just "Irene," began her career as a designer for Hollywood films. She was the executive costume designer at the MGM film studio for most of the 1940s, and opened her own private salon after leaving MGM in 1950. Many of her garments included theatrical touches befitting her experience in film.

This design was exclusive to Frederick & Nelson in Seattle, and was purchased in their elegant Designer Room. In earlier days the department was called the "French Gown Shop," with the understanding that the best, most elite designs came from Paris. But later in the century, particularly after World War II, American designers gained more recognition and were counted among the ranks of the top style leaders.

Previous: The French Gown Shop, before it was renamed the Designer Room, around 1920. This photo was taken shortly after Frederick & Nelson opened their new store on the corner of Pine Street and Fifth Avenue in 1918.

EVENING GOWN WITH LACE BODICE

Tadashi Shoji, New York, maker
Nordstrom, retailer
Jean Chamberlin, owner
2010

At the time she wore this dress, Jean Chamberlin was the vice president and program manager for The Boeing Company's C-17 military transport aircraft program. Chamberlin was drawn to the dress because the color was similar to "Boeing Blue." She wore it to represent Boeing at a gala fundraiser for the 5th Avenue Theater. It was purchased at Nordstrom and made by designer Tadashi Shoji, a red carpet favorite.

Many of the formal gowns donated to MOHAI's collection belonged to wealthy Seattle women who were involved in charity work but often did not have paid employment like their husbands or fathers. Newer acquisitions like this one reflect a cultural shift in roles for women.

The earliest settlers in Seattle had to prioritize practicality. Silks were stored away, and comfortable wool flannels and easy-to-clean cottons became daily staples. Perhaps that early experience never really left.

In the 20th century, like many West Coast communities, Seattle became associated with a relaxed way of living and dressing. Informal styles originally created for sports or at-home wear became increasingly acceptable for a wide variety of situations. A distinct network of manufacturers developed in Seattle to meet a local and national demand for casual clothing. In the 1970s and 1980s, new companies leveraged Seattle's large port and proximity to Asia to produce a higher volume for lower cost. Local casualwear brands flourished. In the 1980s, the Seattle Preline event brought hundreds of fashion buyers to the city to order the latest designs from local firms. The frenzy bumped Seattle up to being the fourth-largest apparel market in the country, behind New York, Los Angeles, and San Francisco.[1] After decades of importing the latest fashions, Seattle began exporting some of the biggest trends of the day around the country and the world.

Seattle's casualwear industry was built off the experience of living here. Companies specialized in relaxed styles for weekend adventures and for people who liked their style served with a little practicality. As the local jeanswear industry took off in the 1980s, a distinct "Northwest Fit" even emerged, one "wider in the leg and a half-inch roomier in the seat and thigh than what people in other parts of the country prefer."[2] Theories varied on the regional preference. Some thought it accommodated large leg muscles built with all the hiking and climbing; others countered that it was based strictly on comfort.

NORTHWEST CASUAL

PRINTED COTTON WRAPPER

Maker unknown

1850s–1860s

It could be argued that Seattle's affinity for casualwear began in its earliest days. The realities of frontier life necessitated practical choices and garments that could serve multiple purposes.

This 19th-century garment is known as a *wrapper*. It features a loose-fitting front that could be worn without a corset, at a time when women wore corsets for nearly every occasion. Wrappers were worn as casual home-wear. They were popular as dressing gowns, as maternity wear, and for nursing mothers. Unlike on most dresses of the day, the front is easy to open, which could accommodate breastfeeding. Patterned cottons like this one, sometimes called *calicos*, were popular goods sold by Seattle founder Arthur A. Denny's local store.[3] They were colorful, could mask stains, and were easy to wash. In his 1857 account of life in the Washington territories, James Swan mentions that blue-and-white patterns were widely popular in Seattle, a favorite of both the Native population and white settlers.[4]

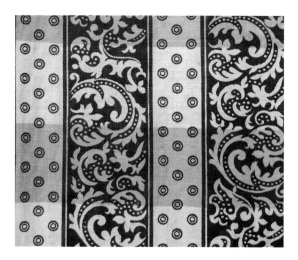

SIDESADDLE RIDING HABIT

Shogren, Portland, maker
ca. 1907

The riding habit is one of the oldest types of sportswear for women. It often incorporates elements of traditional menswear. Habits are usually made of heavy and durable fabrics, and are precisely tailored. They sometimes even have a pair of breeches hidden under the skirt—modesty insurance in the event of being thrown from a horse. This one has a tailored skirt that fits tightly around the legs. The hem appears asymmetrical when standing, but when the wearer is mounted sidesaddle, it hangs straight. In addition to being a starting point for sports and casual clothing, the riding habit was also the earliest incarnation of the women's suit.

This riding habit was an early donation to the museum from the John Collins family. John Collins came to Seattle in the 1860s and was Seattle's fourth mayor. This may have belonged to his wife Angela, or to one of his daughters—Edana or Catherine.

GYM ENSEMBLE

Maker unknown
1930s

This charming seersucker ensemble—with its sporty tie, wraparound skirt, and large green buttons—combines function with stylish accents. It was used as a gym uniform at Seattle's all-girls St. Nicholas School. Seersucker surged in popularity in the 1930s. It was often used as a sport fabric because its waffle-like surface sits slightly away from the skin and allows for air circulation. It is also easy to wash and does not require ironing. The shirt buttons between the legs, which keeps it from pulling out of the skirt even with the most vigorous activity.

Seattle stores sold similar ensembles. They were usually called "sport frocks" and were particularly appropriate for tennis or golf. In an echo of today's *athleisure* trend, one 1933 Frederick & Nelson ad suggested that sporty dresses could also be used for "just loafing."[5]

SHOOTING SWEATER

Sportcraft Knitting, maker
Victor Denny, owner
ca. 1930

This blue-gray sweater was made for wearing while skeet and trap shooting. The leather patch on the shoulder has padding underneath to cushion where the gun rests. At the beginning of the 20th century, sweaters were used almost exclusively for sporting activities. Sweaters slipped into everyday apparel as people grew increasingly attached to the ease and flexibility of comfortable knits, and as sporting activities in turn became more fashionable.

This sweater was made by Sportcraft Knitting in Seattle and worn by Victor Denny. Denny was an avid sportsman and the grandson of Seattle founders David and Louisa Denny. He was a member of the Seattle Gun Club and participated in regional skeet-shooting competitions in the 1920s and 1930s— sometimes against powerhouse sporting couple Christine and Eddie Bauer.

The sweater was part of Sportcraft's line of "Frank Troeh Shooting Jackets." Troeh was a star of the trap-shooting world and lived in Portland, Oregon.

HOSTESS GOWN

John Doyle Bishop, retailer
Marilyn Domoto Webb, owner
1971

The hostess gown sits somewhere between casual and formal, like an evening gown crossed with lounging pajamas. It is made for a woman to wear in her own home—a place for comfort and repose. Like relaxed cotton wrappers of the 19th century, the hostess gown is often loose-fitting and brightly patterned. Yet it also needs to be elegant and memorable, designed for receiving people into the home for a party or event. This one is particularly attention grabbing, as the cut of the fabric creates a large pattern of chevrons on the front and back. The dress was purchased in Seattle from high fashion retailer John Doyle Bishop.

Previous: Marilyn Domoto Webb wore this hostess gown in July of 1971 to host her daughter's first birthday party.
Photo: Eugene Webb

SEATTLE CENTENNIAL SHIRT

Buttnick Manufacturing, maker
1952

This shirt is from a series of patterned shirts and scarves made for Seattle's centennial year, celebrated from November 1951 to November 1952. The print is an interesting collection of Seattle scenes considered iconic during this decade before the Space Needle was built. It includes attractions like the Smith Tower, *Kalakala* ferry, and Lacey V. Murrow Memorial Bridge (I-90 eastbound), as well as images of logging, fishing, sailing, and skiing. It also includes depictions of a totem pole and a woman in a highly inaccurate rendition of Native dress.

This shirt takes inspiration from lightweight, patterned Aloha shirts from Hawaii. Despite the different climate, many Seattle manufacturers drew inspiration from their neighbors in the Pacific. Buttnick Manufacturing was part of Seattle's growing casualwear industry in the midcentury. The company name can still be seen painted on the side of their building at 204 First Avenue South in Pioneer Square.

A couple poses in matching centennial shirts, 1952. The pattern was made in both red and light green.

WORLD'S FAIR PATTERN
TOP AND SKIRT

Foster-Hochberg Manufacturing, maker
1962

"What to wear during the Fair is a fair question," noted the *Seattle Times* in 1961.[6] This shirt and skirt are printed with a delightful pattern that celebrates the 1962 World's Fair in Seattle. The print features images of the Space Needle, Monorail, arches from the US Science Pavilion, and plumes of water spraying from the International Fountain. The garments, sold in stores across the country, are from a series of World's Fair–themed dresses and separates. Pamela Foster and Sailmates were the names of two of Foster-Hochberg's most popular lines.

In the 1950s and 1960s, Foster-Hochberg was one of Seattle's leading clothing manufacturers, specializing in casual sportswear for women and teen girls. Foster-Hochberg met a local demand and sold garments nationally. They found the most success in places that embraced a casual aesthetic similar to Seattle's. One of the company's goals with the World's Fair print was for it to "look as at home in Miami as it would in Seattle."[7]

Gerry Abbott, who also created fashion illustrations for the *Seattle Times*, drew sketches for the pattern.

COTTON DAY DRESS

Marontate-Jones Company, maker
1965–75

Casual dressing is usually more permissive of eye-popping prints than business attire or eveningwear. The print coupled with the cotton fabric and button opening down its front make this dress perfect for vacation or at home on a warm weekend.

The dress was made by the Marontate-Jones Company in Seattle. Founded by Fred Marontate and Frank Jones, the business was one of Seattle's oldest and longest-running manufacturers of women's dresses, outerwear, and separates. The company started in 1921 and continued into the 1980s. The garments were often labeled under the name "Marjone," a shortened version of the company's full name.[8]

JEAN SHIRT AND BELL-BOTTOM PANTS

Brittania Sportswear, maker
Don Holder, owner
1975–79

This ensemble features a denim shirt with embellished pockets and wide bell-bottom pants. The maker, Brittania Sportswear, is credited with bringing *fashion jeans* from London to the United States in the early 1970s. Prior to this, denim was mostly a workwear staple, available in simple, often unisex cuts. Fashion jeans feature different washes and colors, stylized embellishments, and proportions that reflect the style of the time. Their success turned Seattle into a hotspot for a new generation of jeans and casualwear companies.[9]

Brittania's impact on Seattle's casualwear industry went beyond what was made to how it was made. They were one of the earliest clothing companies to manufacture exclusively overseas, leveraging Seattle's proximity to Asia and the less expensive, high-volume production available there. Other companies followed suit, and the presence of local clothing manufacturing began to decline.

Don Holder, who worked in IT at Brittania from 1975 to 1979, purchased these items from the company store.

Detail of shirt pocket. At the height of the fashion jeans craze, a company could live or die by introducing a new color, cut, or unique pocket detail.

I AM A BOY SHIRT

International News, maker
1986

This shirt is unisex; the meaning of the "I am a boy" print can be shaped by the wearer. Influential Seattle-based apparel brand International News made this bold shirt at the height of the local casualwear industry boom.

International News was launched in 1983 when Brittania jeanswear executive Mike Alesko partnered with casualwear giant Shah Safari. Brothers Raj and Akhil Shah launched Shah Safari as teenagers in 1975. The Seattle company designed, manufactured, and imported lightweight, breezy gauze shirts from India. After just eight years in business, Shah Safari owned 24 percent of the national young men's woven shirt market.[10]

Shah Safari and International News have been innovative for decades. In 1985, they opened Zebraclub, a public retail "lab" that showcased and tested emerging global fashion brands and unique merchandising concepts. Today, Shah Safari continues to manage nearly a dozen apparel brands, including Mecca USA, a hip-hop lifestyle brand originally backed by International News and founded by Seattle-born designers who once worked at Zebraclub.[11]

GENERRA

PERCOLOR™

MORPHIC-COLOR-SYSTEM

HYPERCOLOR SWEATSHIRT

Generra Sportswear, maker
1991–92

DENIM SHORTALL

UNIONBAY, maker
1994

Seattle's casualwear industry continued to boom through the 1980s, thanks in part to UNIONBAY and Generra Sportswear. Both were founded in 1980 by former top-level staff from Seattle's Brittania Sportswear.

Generra's aesthetic was youthful and adventurous. By 1989, when Seattle's casualwear companies were leading the national indust Generra was the largest casualwear company in the Puget Sound region.[12] They had a huge hit in 1991 with Hypercolor—a heat-reac fabric whose colors change when warmed. But they overinveste in the fad and filed for bankruptcy in 1992.[13]

UNIONBAY was created to reflect an active and fun Northwest lifestyle.[14] Named after Seattle's Union Bay on Lake Washington, the company is now one of the city's longest-running jeans and casualwear companies. Their tomboyish Shortall of the mid-1990 took inspiration from Seattle's grunge music scene. Designs of oversized, androgynous denim pieces have defined the brand's history. Nostalgia has helped fuel a resurgence in the Shortall's popularity in the late 2010s.

CAMP SHIRT

Tommy Bahama, maker
2003

The silk *camp shirt* is one of Tommy Bahama's earliest and most enduring products. The "camp" collar style may have been originally designed for military fatigues, offering protection against sun and insects in tropical climates. A small loop on the collar's left side can attach to a button on the right, closing the neck. Aloha shirts from Hawaii inspire the fabrics and prints. Tommy Bahama's signature textile includes patterns woven into the fabric and prints on the surface. This one has a geometric woven texture and a blue palm tree print, evoking a cool island breeze. Often, Tommy Bahama's prints reference resort life of the mid-20th century and satirical images such as Santa Claus riding a marlin.

In-house artists create the prints at the company's headquarters in Seattle's South Lake Union neighborhood, quite a distance from the tropical settings their illustrations conjure. Tommy Bahama's founders came from high-level positions at Generra and UNIONBAY. The choice of headquarters owes more to Seattle's existing casualwear industry than to its weather.

MOTHETTE DRESS

Prairie Underground, maker
2008

The "Mothette" dress wraps around the body like a cocoon. It is made of soft French terry cloth and has cording in the bodice, which enables it to adjust to varying torso lengths. Prairie Underground designers Camilla Eckersley and Davora Lindner are five feet five and six feet one, respectively. They are interested in creating garments that suit multiple body types.

Founded in 2004, Prairie Underground incorporates sustainability and ethical business practices into all parts of its production process. The company works to sustain Seattle's existing resources and strengthen its manufacturing, after the local apparel industry has suffered decades of decline. All pieces are made in Seattle, in small editions each season. The sewing contractors all live within 25 minutes of the city. Fabrics are dyed in a sustainable process and frequently made from organic fibers. Prairie Underground is also rethinking the process of inspiration by collaborating with artists and hosting exhibitions in a gallery at their headquarters in Seattle's Georgetown neighborhood.

NEO-TECH DRESS

Buki, maker

2018

The sleek "Neo-Tech" dress is part of the "technical clothing" collection from Seattle company Buki. This dress has a clean, refined look. It is also stretchy and nearly impossible to wrinkle.

Buki works to incorporate the performance of technical fabrics into office-casual chic. Typically, technical fabrics are dipped in a chemical to imbue them with specific properties like moisture wicking and wrinkle-resistance. Buki blends these technologies into the yarns they use—the technical properties are inherent to each thread. The goal is clothing that is comfortable, easy to care for, and casual without sacrificing style and refinement. Buki has its roots not only in Seattle's passion for innovation but also in the city's robust casualwear industry. Co-founder Joey Rodolfo previously worked at several of Seattle's most prominent clothing brands, including UNIONBAY and Tommy Bahama. Co-founder Stacy Bennett is a lifelong Seattleite and has led the marketing efforts for Pacific Northwest brands such as Nordstrom and Amazon.

INNOVATORS AND RULE BREAKERS

Seattle is home to creative problem solvers and nonconformists, people who are up for disrupting the status quo and not afraid to go their own way. Innovations in technology, music, and the arts are the most familiar, but these ideals extend to the domain of clothing as well. What we wear is one of the main ways we express our identity, reflecting our values, our needs, and how we want to present to—and be perceived by—others.

Throughout Seattle's clothing history, people have recognized needs and have created solutions for themselves and others. Sometimes the needs are functional, an improvement to an everyday basic or a lifesaving innovation. Sometimes, there is an artistic vision to bring to the world, a blending of surprising styles or a glamorous creation. In a city not known for its high fashion, the art of crafting exceptional garments and accessories can also be a kind of rebellion. Sometimes, groups or individuals have a belief or identity not represented in mainstream clothing styles and so they innovate. The resulting garments reveal and celebrate the creativity, ingenuity, and diversity of the individuals who make up the region.

Church robe (detail).

SKYLINER DOWN JACKET

Eddie Bauer, maker
1936

During an excursion on the Olympic Peninsula in 1935, local outdoorsman and retailer Eddie Bauer's wool garments became soaked with freezing rain. He started to experience serious signs of hypothermia. After his near-death experience, Bauer set out to make a better coat for cold weather activities, one that would be lighter and warmer and allow for good air circulation. He drew inspiration from his uncle's stories of officers in the Russo-Japanese War who wore down-insulated coats.[1] Bauer's design was a game changer and something new for the US outdoor industry. His puffy down coat used quilting to keep its thickness even throughout. This artifact is the earliest known surviving down jacket made by Bauer. The lightweight and water-resistant "Skyliner" design was patented in 1940.

Eddie Bauer's company has outfitted some of the world's most famous adventurers and mountain climbers. The influential puffy down coat has also scaled the peaks of the fashion world on Paris runways and become a streetwear staple.

Eddie Bauer poses with steelhead trout, 1926. Bauer's experience as an outdoorsman meant he knew the value of good, quality gear.

X-GAITERS

Outdoor Research, maker
1981

In 1980, physicist and mountaineer Ron Gregg found himself in a perilous situation on Alaska's Denali. His partner suffered frostbite and was airlifted out, all because of poorly designed *gaiters*—an accessory worn over the shoe and ankle. Frustrated that a carefully planned trip was derailed by something as simple as a small accessory, Gregg decided to make something better. The result was an insulated gaiter, the "X-Gaiter." From this first inspiration, Seattle-based Outdoor Research (OR) was born the following year.

The "X-Gaiter" sides secure to the foot at the insole with crossed cords, forming an *X*. The design thoroughly insulates the foot and the ankle. The piece features many innovations, including two types of compressible open cell foam for customizing insulation needs. Since 1981, OR has focused on creating the best-possible gear by improving the design of outdoor essentials and pioneering uses for high-performance materials.

Previous: Eddie Bauer Alpine Climbing Guide Dave Hahn on Denali, the highest peak in North America, in 2010. Photo: Ken Sauls

Right: OR founder and lifelong adventurer Ron Gregg on the Anderson Glacier in the Canadian St. Elias Range in 1996. Photo: Kaj Bune Photography

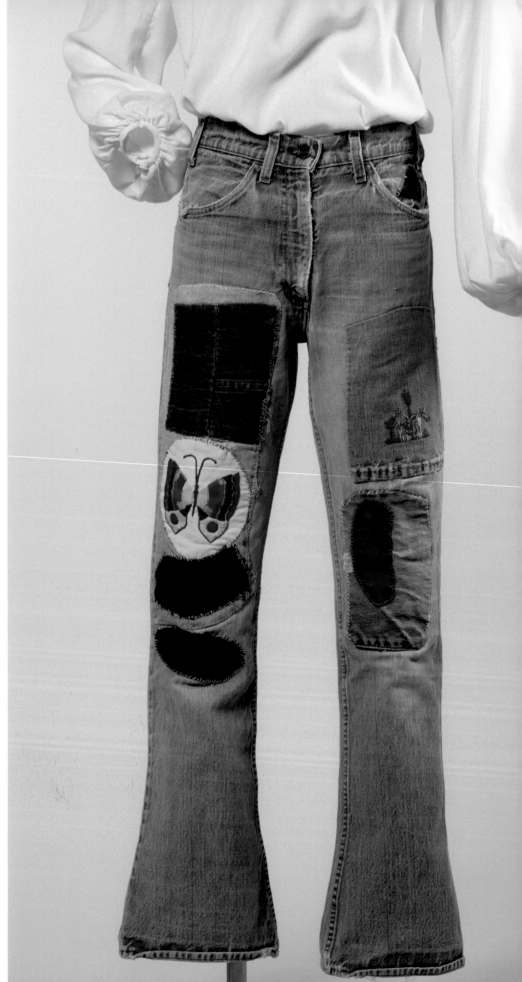

A reveler at Seattle's annual Folklife Festival, 1989. The "hippie" look is relaxed yet rebellious—clothing that favors personal expression over designer trends. It has been a particularly enduring style in Seattle.

DECORATED BELL-BOTTOM PANTS

Janet D. Hesslein, owner
1968–80

Janet Hesslein started wearing these bell-bottom jeans in 1968, and continued to wear and modify them as late as 1980. Hesslein bought the jeans new. As she broke them in and wore them out, she added embroidery and patches.

The hippie counterculture movement of the 1960s was an ideology with an identifiable clothing style. Hippies were suspicious of the fashion industry and rejected the consumerist idea that it was important to constantly buy new things. Making and modifying clothing became a hallmark of hippie style. Patches—traditionally used to extend the life of a ripped or worn garment—were turned into a decorative art form. Hippies also looked to the past and to non-Western fashion for clothing inspiration, including do-it-yourself handicrafts like embroidery, tie-dye, macramé, and crochet. While the movement is most identifiable with San Francisco, it also resonated deeply with Seattleites' tendency toward nonconformity.

GRUNGE

1988–92

There is no fashion moment more associated with Seattle than grunge. The style emerged with the local alternative-rock subculture that started in the late 1980s and exploded nationally in the early 1990s. The look had ingredients of punk style, local workwear, gender-flexibility, and chilly weather practicality, all rolled together with an anti-establishment attitude. Thrift stores were the go-to place for the grunge look. Thrift shopping saved money, but it was also a way to reject flashy 1980s mainstream fashion. Plaid flannels—the workwear of Pacific Northwest timber workers—and worn jeans were plentiful. To keep warm, long johns were added as a visible layer. Initially the style of losers and misfits, the grunge look ended up becoming the height of cool.

As often happens with countercultural styles, the fashion world—high-end and mainstream alike—began to co-opt the look. Marc Jacobs's Spring 1993 grunge collection for Perry Ellis, shown in the fall of 1992, included silk and cashmere flannels. As laughable as the idea of high fashion grunge seemed, it was indicative of how deeply the look resonated with people across the globe. For many Seattleites, it felt like once the style was on the runway and in the pages of *Vogue*, true grunge was dead.

The *Seattle Post-Intelligencer* snapped this photo of Seattleite David Latimer for an article on grunge, 1992. Latimer described how each part of his outfit was either free or purchased secondhand.

WORKMAN KILT

Utilikilts, maker
2006

Utilikilts are all about defiance—defiance against cultural norms and defiance against mainstream menswear. The Utilikilts Company makes garments for men that allow for uninhibited movability. Utilikilts are *unbifurcated* garments, meaning without fabric separation between the legs. Founder Steven "Krash" Villegas took the kilt—usually made of wool tartan—and crossed it with durable workwear fabrics to create a comfortable, utilitarian alternative to pants. The "Workman" is their most iconic model. It is made from heavy, protective cotton canvas, and features roomy back and side pockets plus a retractable side hammer loop called "The Grip."

Villegas established Utilikilts in 2000 after he began selling the hybrid at the Fremont Sunday Market. In Seattle, you can spot Utilikilts everywhere from the city street to job sites, to the opera. Their popularity is resounding proof of the city's nonconformist character.

The online description of the "Workman" says it all: "We can see you now, out there on the job site, headbanging to Slayer, your mullet hanging down to your shoulders, a big honking drill in one hand, a cold beer in the other and all your pants-wearing co-workers sweating their asses off and wondering how you got so damn cool."[2] Photo: Utilikilts

ESSENTIAL SOFT BRA AND 4.5" TRUNKS

TomboyX, maker
2018

The "Essential Soft Bra" and "4.5" Trunks" are two of Seattle-based company TomboyX's most iconic products. Underwear is not usually seen publicly, but it can be just as important as outerwear for creating and projecting confidence. TomboyX is woman and queer owned, and works to create inclusive and empowering products.

TomboyX was launched to meet a need, though a different one than originally expected. Fran Dunaway aimed to create a better button-down shirt for women. The "Tomboy" name for her online fundraising campaign resonated with women and non-binary people, but shirts were not what they wanted. Dunaway and co-founder Naomi Gonzalez quickly heard from so many people who wanted gender-neutral underwear, they shifted direction. At the time, no company made gender-neutral boxer briefs. TomboyX sold out of their first production run before it even shipped. TomboyX's primary mission is to support people in being unapologetically who they were born to be, giving them a first layer of clothing that affirms and celebrates who they are.

In addition to being gender neutral, TomboyX carries all styles in all sizes—XS to 4X. All sizes are priced the same, and designers work with fit models for each size rather than just sizing up small patterns. Photo: TomboyX

MODIFIED EDDIE BAUER SHIRT

Ric Weiland, owner
1990s

One characteristic ingredient of queer style is the subversion of iconic feminine and masculine looks. This shirt addresses the latter. In the Pacific Northwest, the lumberjack is one of our most enduring symbols of rugged masculinity. A check-patterned flannel is synonymous with the vocation. This shirt's owner, Ric Weiland, strategically modified an Eddie Bauer shirt to make it body revealing. The sleeves were removed to highlight his biceps, and alternating squares were cut out to reveal his chest. Weiland wore the shirt to a flannel-themed LGBTQ party in Seattle.

Weiland was the first lead programmer for Microsoft. He retired at age 35 in 1988. As the value of his stock holdings grew, Weiland increasingly devoted himself to philanthropy. Between the $21.5 million donated before his death in 2006 and the $170 million bequeathed after, Weiland made a significant national impact on HIV research, LGBTQ legal rights, and the presence of gay-straight alliances and anti-bullying policies in schools.[3]

Upper: Ric Weiland at a Halloween party, 1983. Photo: Richard William Weiland Papers (SC0855). Department of Special Collections and University Archives, Stanford Libraries, Stanford, CA

Lower: Weiland with Bill Gates at a conference in New York in 1976. Photo: Richard William Weiland Papers (SC0855). Department of Special Collections and University Archives, Stanford Libraries, Stanford, CA

CHURCH ROBE AND HAT

Flo Wells, maker
Rev. Dr. Samuel B. McKinney, owner
1970s–1980s

This robe and hat belonged to Rev. Dr. Samuel B. McKinney, civil rights leader and pastor of Mount Zion Baptist Church. As a highly visible public figure, McKinney was conscious of the meaning behind his clothing and intentionally forged his identity as an African American leader in Seattle.

This robe is made of adinkra cloth from Ghana. Adinkra is also the name for the symbols printed on the cloth—each symbol has a distinct meaning or associated proverb. The main repeating symbol on this robe is the *Mmusuyidee*, which signifies spiritual strength and the removal of evil. The fabric was probably sewn into a robe in Seattle. It is lined in blue polyester and has a label from a home seamstress, which reads "Custom Made by Flo Wells"—likely a member at Mount Zion Baptist Church. The garment combines a West African spiritual tradition with McKinney's dedicated support of African American businesses and love of his Pacific Northwest community.

Rev. McKinney on March 9, 1958. Mount Zion Baptist Church is home to one of the oldest and largest African American congregations in Washington State. The Sanctuary Choir is visible in the background.

COAT WITH FULL SKIRT

Clara B. White, maker
1960s–1980s

Seamstress Clara B. White created and wore this stately gray coat. The coat is embellished with lines of ribbon and velvet diamonds appliqued onto the surface, and features a burgundy lining. White came to Seattle in the 1920s and owned a duplex on 22nd Avenue. The First African Methodist Episcopal Church on 14th Avenue has a wing named after her—she was a Sunday school teacher there for 60 years.

While little is known about Clara B. White's designs, it is likely that sewing was her business and the surrounding Central District community was her clientele. Home seamstresses represent a large pool of under-recognized labor in the fashion world. They sometimes work out of their homes as a small design business, do contract work for larger companies, or create garments for family and friends—or all three.

DRESS WITH KIMONO SLEEVES

Richmond of Seattle, maker
1970s

Robert Richmond was an independent designer who made custom dresses for an elite Seattle clientele under the label Richmond of Seattle. The easy elegance of this dress shows many hallmarks of his style. "I like a V-neck, a long sleeve, an easy-fitting waist, and a flared skirt," he once said.[4] Richmond didn't sketch his designs, preferring instead to get inspired by draping and experimenting with fabric on a form.[5] As one client said, "He loves to see women in clothes that flow and move in a sweep of color."[6]

Richmond made a name for himself as an independent, high-end designer in Seattle, amid the city's growing casualwear industry. In 1980, his creations started at $150 and went up to $2,000, prices comparable to Frederick & Nelson's Designer Room and boutiques like John Doyle Bishop. He employed two seamstresses and had a small atelier downtown, across the street from the Washington Athletic Club.

EVENING GOWN AND COAT

Howard Blair, maker
1959

This exquisite gold gown and coat are made with over 50 yards of silk. The designer, Howard Blair, created it for an event hosted by the Fashion Group of Seattle to promote trade with Japan.[7] Despite the fresh memory of World War II, Seattle built a friendly relationship with Japan in the 1950s. The silk from this dress is from Kobe, Seattle's sister city since 1957.

Blair started designing in high school, when he made theater costumes and prom dresses for friends. Working out of his family home, he became a go-to designer for local and national pageant-queen dresses, wedding gowns, and evening attire. In 1958, just eight years into his career, he was reported to already have made 600 dresses for Seattle clients.[8] Blair's designs were worn by those who wanted to stand out. To make sure this dress would grab attention—as if the noticeable embellishments would not suffice—Blair attached small bells to the interior of both pieces.

Blair's illustration of the gown and jacket, 1961. His dresses use high-quality materials and are so firmly structured that one client joked that it would take a chisel and hammer to take the dress apart. Photo: Howard Blair

EVENING HAT OR FASCINATOR

Ethel Young, maker
1950s

STRIPED TOQUE

John Eaton, maker
ca. 1963

These whimsical hats are examples of the inventive art of *millinery,* or hat making. Seattle has a particularly strong tradition of millinery thanks in part to Ethel Young and John Eaton. Both taught generations of students, who in turn taught others.

Ethel Young was sometimes referred to as the "dean of Seattle milliners." She opened her business in 1934 and at one time employed 30 women. As Young once described her work, "It takes a couple of days to make a hat. You have to make your frame, then your material. You sew it on by hand. Then you block your lining. It takes a person about 10 years to even learn. But once you are in it, you just don't want to quit."[9]

Seattleite John Eaton opened his millinery shop in 1950. His designs range from the fantastical to the practical; he often made hats to match an outfit. Later he started designing clothing too, so he could dress a client from head to toe.[10]

BLACK AND WHITE ROSE HAT

Wayne Wichern, maker
1995

PEACE FEDORA

Sonia Wooten-Gill, maker
2017

Seattle's millinery community has stayed strong into the 21st century—thanks in part to a culture built on collaboration rather than competition. The Millinery Artisan Guild of the Pacific Northwest organizes group shows and helps local milliners share resources. Wayne Wichern and Sonia Wooten-Gill are two members of the guild and examples of the enduring community.

Leaves and flowers are a favorite inspiration for Seattle milliner Wayne Wichern. This hat is an adaptation of a petal pattern made by John Eaton, Wichern's teacher and mentor. Wichern now teaches millinery classes in Seattle and around the country.

Sonia Wooten-Gill founded the Faye Woo Signature Collection after taking classes from Wichern and others. African American milliners sometimes specialize in church hats, but Wooten-Gill intends her designs to be worn all week. Wooten-Gill formed felt into this fedora shape by hand. She added the ribbon because she felt our era needed a message of peace.

SALISH PATTERN WOOL BLANKET

Louie Gong, maker
Eighth Generation, maker and retailer
2018

In 2015, Seattle-based Eighth Generation became the first Native-owned company to produce wool blankets. While the blankets can be used as décor, they are designed to be worn as honor gifts—wrapped around the shoulders of someone recognized by their community for an achievement or contribution. Honor blanket ceremonies vary; they are a long-held tradition for tribes across the US. Louie Gong (Nooksack), Eighth Generation's founder, designed the "Salish Pattern" Wool Blanket. The pattern uses the same design elements in an irregular sequence rather than a simple repeat. The blanket design pays homage to Coast Salish weaving traditions that stretch back hundreds of years.

Anchored by the tagline "Inspired Natives, not 'Native-inspired,'" Eighth Generation provides a strong, ethical alternative to companies that profit off fake Native art through its artist-centric approach and 100 percent Native-designed products. They directly contract a variety of Native artists, creating designs for many tribes and non-Native consumers alike.

Squamish carver Peter Gong made this custom wolf pin closure used with the blanket. Photo: Louie Gong

135

NOTES

NATURE AND PLACE

1   "Dr. Belle Stevens," *Seattle Daily Times*, September 6, 1960, 28.
2   Paola Antonelli and Michelle Millar Fisher, *Items: Is Fashion Modern* (New York: Museum of Modern Art, 2017), 129. Exhibition catalog.
3   "Timeline," Mountain Safety Research website, accessed November 1, 2018, aspdotnetstorefront .cascadedesigns.com/msr/timeline.
4   "About Us," Mountain Safety Research website, accessed November 1, 2018, msrgear.com/about.
5   *Complete Catalog and Price List* (Seattle, WA: C. C. Filson Co., 1914).
6   Winifred Black, "Women Are Not Angels," *Seattle Daily Times*, July 10, 1919, 6.
7   Marion O. Ferriss, "One Man's Work Clothes Another's Weakness," *Seattle Daily Times*, August 3, 1930, 9.
8   Seattle Woolen Company ad, *Seattle Daily Times*, January 4, 1948, 30.
9   Bud Livesley, "Stretch: A Seattle Firm's Togs Have It," *Seattle Daily Times Magazine*, January 26, 1964, 1–2, 10–11.
10 Nicole Hjorth, "Miss Skiwear," *Seattle Times*, February 13, 1973, B1.
11 "Local Labels No Longer Say 'Made in the USA,'" *Seattle Times*, June 19, 1984, C1-2.
12 "John S. Graham, Pioneer Seattle Merchant, Dies," *Seattle Daily Times*, August 16, 1924, 1.
13 "Personal," *Seattle Daily Times*, August 9, 1899, 8.
14 Advertisement for J.S. Graham, *Seattle Daily Times*, December 21, 1899, 5.
15 Marilyn Kirkby, "Bishop Is Remembered as Flamboyant and Kind," *Seattle Times*, October 22, 1980, C5
16 Dorothy Neighbors [pseud.], "Reversible Coat," *Seattle Daily Times*, May 7, 1962, 17.

GROWTH AND ASPIRATION

1   Gene Balk, "114,000 More People: Seattle Now Decade's Fastest-Growing Big City in All of US," *Seattle Times*, posted May 24, 2017, and accessed September 14, 2018, seattletimes.com/seattle-news/data/114000-more-people-seattle-now-this-decades-fastest-growing-big-city-in-all-of-united-states/7.
2   Cassandra Tate, "Gold in the Pacific Northwest," Historylink, posted December 6, 2004, and accessed January 31, 2018, historylink.org/File/7162.
3   Fred Poyner IV, "C. C. Filson Company," Historylink, posted November 25, 2015, and accessed October 26, 2018, historylink.org/File/11150.
4   Robert Spector and Patrick D. McCarthy, *The Nordstrom Way: The Inside Story of America's #1 Customer Service Company* (New York: Wiley, 1995), 42-44.
5   Nordstrom ad, *Seattle Daily Times*, January 19, 1912, 4.
6   "Frye's Opera House," The Early History of Seattle Theatre in Seattle, accessed November 1, 2018, seattletheaterhistory.org/collections/theatres -places/fryes-opera-house.
7   "MacDougall-Southwick 80 Years Old," *Seattle Daily Times*, October 30, 1955, 15.
8   "To Send Buyers to Europe," *Seattle Daily Times*, April 21, 1907, 31.
9   James R. Warren, "Bon Marche Department Store," Historylink, posted September 18, 1999, updated April 27, 2006, and accessed November 1, 2018, historylink.org/File/1676.
10 Deborah McNally, "Zoë Dusanne (1884-1972)," Blackpast, accessed October 30, 2018, blackpast .org/aaw/dusanne-zoe-1884-1972.
11 Jo Ann Ridley, *Zoë Dusanne: An Art Dealer Who Made a Difference* (McKinleyville, CA: Fithian Press, 2011), xiv.
12 Don Duncan, "An Extraordinary Life—Her Life as a Social Butterfly Not Enough for Plestcheeff," *Seattle Times*, November 2, 1990, E1.
13 Meredith Clausen, "Oral History Interview with Paul Thiry, September 15-16, 1983," Archives of American Art, accessed October 29, 2018, aaa.si.edu/ collections/interviews/oral-history-interview-paul -thiry-11659#transcript.
14 Sybil McCain, "Fifth Avenue Moves Westward," *Seattle Woman Magazine*, March 1925, 16.
15 "To Send Buyers to Europe," 31.
16 "Shop Has Birthday," *Seattle Daily Times*, March 16, 1920, 2.
17 June Weir, "The Fashionable Bishop," *Women's Wear Daily*, December 10, 1968, 10.
18 "John Doyle Bishop—A Fashion Leprechaun," *Seattle Times*, March 20, 1980, F4.
19 "Ruth B. Clayburgh, 92, Longtime Patron of Arts," *Seattle Times*, October 3, 2002, B2.
20 Dorothy Neighbors [pseud.], "Symphoneve Dinner Dance Has Colorful Florentine Air," *Seattle Daily Times*, October 14, 1962, S11.

Previous: Model posing in gold dress by Seattle designer Malorie Nelson, 1978.

NORTHWEST CASUAL

1   Marilyn Kirkby, "Pre-Line Shows Draw Lines for Holiday Wear," *Seattle Times*, July 26, 1984, G1.
2   Carol Pucci, "Seattle's Jeans Machine," *Pacific Magazine, Seattle Times*, September 19, 1982, 6–14.
3   Arthur Armstrong Denny, Field Book (1850–1854, 1858. Accession No. 2343-003: Arthur Armstrong Denny papers, 1844–1896, Box 1, folder 4).
4   James G. Swan, *The Northwest Coast, or Three Years' Residence in Washington Territory* (New York: Harper & Bros., 1857), 154.
5   Frederick & Nelson ad, *Seattle Daily Times*, June 28, 1933, 7.
6   "World's Fair Fashions Geared Toward the Space Age," *Seattle Daily Times*, December 14, 1961, 35.
7   "World's Fair Fashions," 35.
8   Sally Gene Mahony, "Distributers Here Are Happy," *Seattle Times*, January 10, 1981, C7.
9   Pucci, "Seattle's Jeans Machine," 6–14.
10 Monica Soto Ouchi, "Shah Safari Still on Top of Trends After 30 Years," *Seattle Times*, October 29, 2006.
11 Cynthia Rose, "The Mecca Guys Are Back to Launch a New, Urbane Line," *Seattle Times*, February 28, 1997.
12 "Bid Reported for Generra," *Seattle Times*, March 21, 1989, F7.
13 Sylvia Wieland Nogaki, "Fast Growth Led to Woes at Generra," *Seattle Times*, August 12, 1992, B4.
14 Steve Wilhelm, "Importer Surges: Apparel Firm's UNIONBAY Line is Hot," *Puget Sound Business Journal*, posted February 2, 2003, and accessed December 14, 2018, bizjournals.com/seattle/stories/2003/02/03/story1.html.

INNOVATORS AND RULE BREAKERS

1   Robert Spector, *The Legend of Eddie Bauer* (Lyme, CO: Greenwich Publishing Group, 1994), 37.
2   "The Workman Utilikilt," Utilikilts website, accessed October 29, 2018, utilikilts.com/the-workman-utilikilt.html.
3   Nina Shapiro, "Microsoft Pioneer Ric Weiland's Huge Bequest Changed Science, Society," *Seattle Times*, posted January 7, 2017, and accessed December 14, 2018, seattletimes.com/seattle-news/health/microsoft-pioneers-huge-bequest-changed-science-society.
4   "Robert Richmond, Authentic Original," *Seattle Times*, April 27, 1980, E1.
5   Nicole Hjorth, "Potpourri," *Seattle Times*, February 8, 1977, D3.
6   "Robert Richmond," E1.
7   "Japanese Textiles Will Be Displayed by Fashion Group," *Seattle Daily Times*, March 23, 1959, 32.
8   "Seattle Designer, Too, Considered Chemise 'Terrible,'" *Seattle Daily Times*, December 3, 1958, 49.
9   "Seattle's Vanishing Craftspeople," *Seattle Times, Pictorial Magazine*, April 23, 1978, 17.
10 Ferdinand M. De Leon, "John Eaton, Hat Maker, Designer, Who Shared His Skill with Others," *Seattle Times*, April 3, 1991, F3.

SELECTED BIBLIOGRAPHY

Artifact records, Museum of History & Industry, Seattle, WA.

Berg, Clara Evangeline. "Only Fashion Spoken Here: John Doyle Bishop in Seattle, 1947–1980." M.A. thesis, Fashion Institute of Technology, 2011.

Korsmo, Elizabeth. "Not Really So Primitive as One Might Be Led to Believe: Interpreting Early Seattle Dress." M.A. thesis, University of Washington, 2018.

Le Zote, Jennifer. *From Goodwill to Grunge: A History of Secondhand Styles and Alternative Economies* (Chapel Hill: University of North Carolina Press, 2017).

Mears, Patricia. *Expedition: Fashion from the Extreme*. New York: Thames & Hudson, 2017. Exhibition catalog.

Phinney, Susan. "Seattle is a Fashion Industry Player." Seattle Business Magazine, March 2012, and accessed December 14, 2018, seattlebusinessmag.com/article/seattles-fashion-industry-player.

Poneman, Jonathan. "Grunge and Glory," *Vogue*, December 1992.

Spector, Robert. *The Legend of Eddie Bauer*. Lyme, CO: Greenwich Publishing Group, 1994.

———. *More Than a Store: Frederick & Nelson, 1890–1990*. Bellevue, WA: Documentary Book Publishers Corp., 1990.

Whitley, Lauren. *Hippie Chic*. Boston: Museum of Fine Arts with MFA Publications, 2013. Exhibition catalog.

Zak, Marilyn Anne. "Seattle's Place in the Fashion World." M.A. thesis, University of Washington, 1965.

CREDITS

PAGE 11
Heavy canvas poncho
1961.2244.5 C-2013
Gift of Miss Della J. Patch

PAGE 12
Lloyd and Mary Anderson, 1946
2000.107.008.02.02
Seattle Post-Intelligencer
Collection

PAGE 13
Hiking boots
2000.55.1
Gift of Leila C. Martin

PAGE 15
Early Gore-Tex rain jacket
2003.32.1
Gift of Mary Ann Dobratz

PAGE 16
Hunting jacket and breeches
[Jacket]
1960.2139. C-712
Gift of Mrs. Charles Craig
[Pants]
1963.3008.5 C-975
Gift of Mrs. Paul C. Harper

PAGE 19
Hiking outfit
1961.2417.7 C-782
Gift of Mrs. Trevett Green

PAGE 20
Skiers at Snoqualmie Pass, 1938
PI26875
Seattle Post-Intelligencer
Collection

PAGE 23
Wool ski ensemble
1976.6342. C-2251
Gift of Francis Seeley (Byron L.)
Nevilier

PAGE 24
Ski stretch pants, 1983
2000.107.061.03.05
Seattle Post-Intelligencer
Collection

PAGE 25
One-piece ski suit
2018.45.1
MOHAI Collection

PAGE 27
Wool evening coat
C-108
MOHAI Collection

PAGE 29
Overcoat with cape
1977.6535. C-2346
Gift of John Doyle Bishop

PAGE 30
*Republic of China Pavilion, Seattle
World's Fair, 1962*
1987.59.131.90
Robert D. Ashley Century 21
Collection

PAGE 32
"Fairweather" raincoat
1992.2
Gift of Babbie Hellyer

PAGE 34
"Colette" raincoat
2018.46.1
Gift of Miriam Reynolds Rigby

PAGE 39
Wool "Mackinaw Cruiser" jacket
2013.42.1
Gift of Filson

PAGE 40
Wallin & Nordstrom, ca. 1901
1986.5.12080.1
Seattle Post-Intelligencer
Collection

PAGE 41
Heeled boots
1973.5687.3
Gift of Mrs. Leona M. Bourke

PAGE 43
Cellular automata knit scarf
2018.66.1
Gift of KnitYak

PAGE 45
Evening bonnet
1972.5374.56 M-624
Gift of Mrs. Barbara B. (MacMillan)
Pringle

PAGE 46
Toklas, Singerman & Co., ca. 1888
Lib1991.5.41
William S. Newton Photographs

PAGE 47
Chiffon and taffeta dress
1975.5995.9 C-2095
Gift of Miss Katharine Lund

PAGE 48
Dress and jacket ensemble
2016.106.1
Gift of Beth Koutsky

PAGE 49
Josephine Nordhoff, ca. 1900
2009.20.216.1
Bon Marché Collection

PAGE 51
Delphos gown
1963.3001.1 C-972
Gift of Zoë Dusanne via Fashion
Group of Seattle

PAGE 53
Velvet evening gown
1971.5218.3 C-1689
Gift of Mrs. William E. Marten

ACKNOWLEDGMENTS

The *Seattle Style: Fashion/Function* exhibit on view at the Museum of History & Industry May 4 to October 14, 2019 is presented by Nordstrom.

Additional generous support was provided by Eddie Bauer, 4Culture, and Lead Donors to the MOHAI Exhibits Fund: Elizabeth Ruth Wallace Trust, Peggy and George Corley, Maureen Frisch, Ted and Linda Johnson, Mary Ann and John Mangels, Tom McQuaid, Glen and Alison Milliman, Gary and Susan Neumann, Chuck Nordhoff, Pepper Family Fund, Mike Repass, and the True-Brown Foundation.

This catalog benefited from valuable input from Ann Poulson and Deborah Vandermar; supplementary research by Elizabeth Korsmo, Pam McClusky, and Marguerite Paul; copyediting by Meka Manchak and Carrie Wicks; mannequin dressing by Kirsten Olsen, Regan Samul, and Kayla Trail; conservation work by liana Lopez Salado; photography by Brady Harvey; and supporting photography by Stephanie Ikeda.

Significant contributions to this project were also made by MOHAI staff, the Board of Trustees, and the *Seattle Style* Community Advisory Committee, whose members include:

Patrick Angus, Marios
Colin Berg, Eddie Bauer
Jessica Burstein, University of Washington
Suk Chai, SCHAI/Mode Legion Design Group
Ron Chew
Jill Donnelly, Baby & Company
Brian Fisher, Filson
Red Godfrey, Nordstrom
Louie Gong and Serene Lawrence, Eighth Generation
Jeff Greenwell, Outdoor Research
Andrew Hoge, *Seattle Magazine*
Linda Johnson, community volunteer
Shannon Kelly, Trendscaping
Melissa Kessenich and Kent Rogers, Butch Blum
Tanya Knannlein, School of Apparel Design & Development at Seattle Central
Davora M. Lindner, Prairie Underground
Sydney Mintle, Gossip & Glamour
Erin Moyer and Suzanne Alberti, Laird Norton Wealth Management
Carol Munro, MOHAI Board of Trustees
Hisako Nakaya, emeritus faculty, School of Apparel Design & Development at Seattle Central
Bradley O'Brien, Tommy Bahama
Steve Ritchey and Jacklyn Story, UNIONBAY
Deborah Ross, Pine Street Group
Detra Segar, Detra Segar Consulting
Krista Schreiber and Jill Price-Crawley, Washington State University Apparel Merchandising, Design & Textiles Advisory Board
Raj Shah and Akhil Shah, Shah Safari and International News
Judy Sourakli, formerly Henry Art Gallery
Sable Talley, Fashion Group International Seattle
Amy Tipton, Sassafras
Deborah Vandermar
Tracey Wickersham, Visit Seattle
Luly Yang, Luly Yang Couture

Published in conjunction with the exhibit *Seattle Style: Fashion/Function*, organized by the Museum of History & Industry (MOHAI), May to October 2019.

Support for this project provided in part by a grant from the Institute of Museum and Library Services. The views, findings, conclusions, or recommendations expressed in this publication do not necessarily represent those of the Institute of Museum and Library Services.

ISBN: 978-0-692-04350-9

Design: Beth Koutsky
Editors: Clara Berg and Isabelle Heyward
Publication Coordinator: Isabelle Heyward

Distributed by the University of Washington Press.
Print and color management by iocolor, Seattle
Printed in China at Artron Color Printing Ltd.

Unless otherwise noted, all photos courtesy of MOHAI

Front cover: Heavy canvas poncho (detail).
Title page: Evening gown with lace overlay (detail).
Contents page: Evening hat or fascinator (detail).
Back cover: Silk evening gown (detail).

860 Terry Ave North, Seattle, WA 98109
MOHAI.org